NBA's TOP 10 ROOKIES

BY WILL GRAVES

→ NBA's TOP 10

SportsZone
An Imprint of Abdo Publishing
abdopublishing.com

abdopublishing.com

Published by Abdo Publishing, a division of ABDO, PO Box 398166, Minneapolis, Minnesota 55439. Copyright © 2019 by Abdo Consulting Group, Inc. International copyrights reserved in all countries. No part of this book may be reproduced in any form without written permission from the publisher. SportsZone™ is a trademark and logo of Abdo Publishing.

Printed in the United States of America, North Mankato, Minnesota
022018
092018

THIS BOOK CONTAINS RECYCLED MATERIALS

Cover Photo: Rich Pedroncelli/AP Images
Interior Photos: Rick Havner/AP Images, 4–5; Michael S. Green/AP Images, 7; Michael Kim/AP Images, 9; AP Images, 10–11, 13, 23, 25; John Swart/AP Images, 14–15; David Zalubowski/AP Images, 16; Michael Conroy/AP Images, 17; Chris O'Meara/AP Images, 19; Rusty Kennedy/AP Images, 20, 21; Rich Clarkson/Sports Illustrated/Getty Images, 24; Manny Millan /Sports Illustrated/Getty Images, 26

Editor: Patrick Donnelly
Series Designer: Craig Hinton

Library of Congress Control Number: 2017962581

Publisher's Cataloging-in-Publication Data

Names: Graves, Will, author.
Title: NBA's top 10 rookies / by Will Graves.
Other titles: NBA's top ten rookies
Description: Minneapolis, Minnesota : Abdo Publishing, 2019. | Series: NBA's top 10 | Includes online resources and index.
Identifiers: ISBN 9781532114540 (lib.bdg.) | ISBN 9781532154379 (ebook)
Subjects: LCSH: Rookie basketball players--Juvenile literature. | Basketball--Records--United States--Juvenile literature. | Basketball--History--Juvenile literature. | National Basketball Association--Juvenile literature.
Classification: DDC 796.323--dc23

TABLE OF CONTENTS

INTRODUCTION 4

10 6
09 8
08 10
07 12
06 14
05 16
04 18
03 20
02 22
01 24

HONORABLE MENTIONS 28
GLOSSARY 30
MORE INFORMATION 31
ONLINE RESOURCES 31
INDEX 32
ABOUT THE AUTHOR 32

INTRODUCTION

In professional sports leagues such as the National Basketball Association (NBA), a first-year player is called a "rookie." Many rookies spend their first seasons trying to get used to playing with the best players in the world. Most end up watching from the bench while the older players get most of the playing time.

But some rookies jump right into the fire and make an instant impact. Some use their speed. Some take advantage of their size. Some rely on their basketball smarts. And some succeed thanks to a little bit of everything.

Though the players featured in this book ended up taking different paths during their careers, they all began as rookies. They just didn't play like rookies. They played like stars who didn't worry about being the new kid on the block. Instead, they took over the block.

10

Allen Iverson brought his fearless brand of basketball to the NBA in 1996.

ALLEN IVERSON

The Philadelphia 76ers had fallen on hard times in the mid-1990s. They needed a spark to change their fortunes. Thanks to a lucky bounce of a ping-pong ball, they wound up with an all-time game-changer.

The 76ers won the NBA Draft Lottery in 1996 and used the top pick to select speedy guard Allen Iverson from Georgetown University. One of Iverson's many nicknames was "The Answer." A family friend gave Iverson that nickname because Iverson was going to answer the NBA's need for new stars.

Though he stood only 6 feet tall, Iverson's height did not stop him from coming up big against the NBA's best. His quickness made it nearly impossible for players to defend him.

Iverson won the NBA Rookie of the Year Award for the 1996–97 season after averaging 23.5 points, 7.5 assists, and 4.1 rebounds per game. He set a rookie record by scoring at least 40 points in five straight games.

Iverson welcomed the challenge of making Philadelphia a winner again. He rose to the challenge when the last-place 76ers squared off against Michael Jordan and the NBA champion Chicago Bulls late in the year. Iverson finished with 37 points that night. The Bulls ended up narrowly winning the game, but Iverson had sent a message: he truly was the "Answer" to Philadelphia's prayers.

SHORT-CIRCUITED

At 6 feet tall, Allen Iverson was one of the smallest top draft picks in NBA history. The shortest player taken No. 1 overall was Gene Melchiorre. The Baltimore Bullets selected the 5-foot-8 guard in the 1951 draft. But Melchiorre never played in the NBA. He was banned for cheating during his college career at Bradley University.

LeBron James immediately changed the fortunes of the Cleveland Cavaliers.

LEBRON JAMES

LeBron James was already famous when he arrived in the NBA. He made the cover of *Sports Illustrated* while he was still in high school. The headline screamed "The Chosen One." Nike paid James $90 million to wear its gear when he said he was going to the NBA. At 6 feet 8 inches tall, he had the size of a power forward, but he could pass like a point guard.

James grew up in Akron, Ohio. That's approximately an hour south of Cleveland. The NBA's Cleveland Cavaliers were one of the worst teams in the league when they used the top pick in the 2003 draft to take James. The hometown kid immediately changed Cleveland's fortunes. The Cavaliers became the hottest ticket in town as fans turned out to see if the 18-year-old kid could really play.

James ended up taking the NBA by storm. He scored 25 points in his first game. And he was just getting started. James averaged 20.9 points, 5.9 assists, and 5.5 rebounds during his rookie season.

More important, the Cavaliers won 35 games that first season. That's more than twice the number of games they won the year before James joined the team.

During that electric first season, he proved to be better than the hype. By the end of his rookie year, the "Chosen One" had a new nickname: "King James." And the King would rule the NBA for years to come.

PREPS TO PROS

LeBron James is one of three players in NBA history to be selected with the top pick in the draft straight out of high school. Kwame Brown went No. 1 to the Washington Wizards in 2001, and the Orlando Magic used the top pick of the 2004 draft on Dwight Howard. The NBA changed the rules in 2006, declaring that players had to be at least one year out of high school before they were eligible for the draft.

08

WALT BELLAMY

Big men ruled in the early days of the NBA. First came Minneapolis Lakers star George Mikan in the early 1950s. Bill Russell in Boston and Wilt Chamberlain in Philadelphia soon followed.

The Chicago Packers pinned their hopes on Walt Bellamy being the NBA's next great center. They selected the 6-foot-11 Indiana University star with the first pick in the 1961 draft, hoping he could turn the team into a winner.

Bellamy came to the Packers after helping the United States win a gold medal in basketball at the 1960 Summer Olympics. Team USA's roster was filled with future stars such as Jerry West and Oscar Robertson. But while Robertson and West went on to win NBA championships, Bellamy's career took a different path.

The Packers were an expansion team, and their first season in the NBA was a rough one. Chicago went 18–62, the worst record in the league. Most of the players on the team were young and lacked NBA experience.

The one thing the Packers did have that season was Bellamy. While his teammates had trouble playing in the NBA, Bellamy looked like he had been there for years.

Rookie Walt Bellamy, *left*, shakes hands with another star center of his era, Wilt Chamberlain.

Bellamy averaged 31.6 points in 1961–62, the third-highest scoring average by a rookie in league history. Bellamy could also crash the boards. He averaged 19.0 rebounds during his first season, also the third-best total ever for a rookie.

While the team struggled, Bellamy's play caught the attention of others. He was named to the All-Star team and ended up as the NBA Rookie of the Year.

Like Mikan, Russell, and Chamberlain, Bellamy ruled the court. He just never won nearly as much as the big men who came before him.

07

Kareem Abdul-Jabbar shows off his skyhook as a rookie against the New York Knicks.

KAREEM ABDUL-JABBAR

Long before he came to the NBA, Kareem Abdul-Jabbar was changing the game of basketball. The 7-foot-2 center was so dominant during his sophomore year at the University of California, Los Angeles (UCLA) in 1967 that dunking was outlawed in the college game.

All that did was make Abdul-Jabbar an even better player. The rules change led him to come up with a shot that was just as hard to stop. He called it the "skyhook." Abdul-Jabbar put his back to the basket, then turned to his left or his right. He then lifted the ball high in the air and flipped it toward the hoop. The shot seemed to drop out of the sky and into the basket.

The skyhook was impossible to stop. So was Abdul-Jabbar. He led UCLA to three straight national titles in college. He was just what the Milwaukee Bucks were looking for in the 1969 NBA draft.

The Bucks and the Phoenix Suns tied for the worst record in the NBA in 1969. The league broke the tie by flipping a coin. The Bucks ended up winning a coin toss that changed NBA history.

Abdul-Jabbar finished second in the NBA in scoring as a rookie, averaging 28.8 points per game. He averaged 14.5 rebounds per game as the Bucks became instant winners. Milwaukee reached the playoffs for

NEW NAME, SAME GAME

Kareem Abdul-Jabbar grew up in New York City as Lew Alcindor. He changed his name in 1971 for religious reasons. Kareem Abdul-Jabbar means "noble, powerful servant."

the first time. Abdul-Jabbar's star power and signature shot made the NBA popular in its new city.

06

MICHAEL JORDAN

The Chicago Bulls held the third pick in the 1984 draft. They were high on guard Michael Jordan, who starred in college at the University of North Carolina.

Other teams wanted Jordan too. So they asked the Bulls if they were willing to trade the pick. The Philadelphia 76ers even offered superstar Julius Erving to the Bulls.

Chicago held on to the pick. That turned out to be a smart decision.

Jordan changed basketball forever. Before he came to the NBA, the game revolved around big men in the middle. Jordan was a 6-foot-6 guard who could soar over the big guys on his way to the basket.

Jordan hit the shot that gave North Carolina the 1982 national championship, but he was never a big scorer in college because Tar Heels coach Dean Smith used so many players.

That wasn't a problem in Chicago. The Bulls decided to let Jordan loose in the NBA. The player who became known as "Air Jordan" took off. He scored 37 points in his third game, and he was just getting started. In his ninth game, he pumped in 45 against the San Antonio Spurs. His 49 points against the

> Michael Jordan shows off his acrobatic moves as a rookie.

Detroit Pistons were a Bulls rookie record. Jordan made the All-Star team and finished as the NBA's third-leading scorer, averaging 28.2 points per game.

    Chicago made the playoffs in Jordan's first season but lost in the opening round. That didn't matter. Jordan's spectacular play proved the Bulls made the right choice by picking him. His rookie season set the table for a career that included six NBA titles and five Most Valuable Player (MVP) Awards. After that, the only question was how Jordan ever fell to third in the draft.

05

Tim Duncan throws down a dunk against the Indiana Pacers during his rookie season.

TIM DUNCAN

The San Antonio Spurs picked the perfect time to be terrible. All-Star center David Robinson suffered back and foot injuries that forced him to miss all but six games of the 1996–97 season. The Spurs went on to win just 20 games that season.

That meant San Antonio ended up with a chance to land the top pick in the NBA Draft. Teams were scrambling for a shot at Wake Forest University center Tim Duncan. The Spurs won the draft lottery and made the obvious choice. Duncan was "old school" by NBA standards. He grew up on St. Croix in the US Virgin Islands, a place hardly known for creating basketball players. He actually wanted to become an Olympic swimmer but changed his mind after a storm destroyed the only Olympic-sized pool on the island of St. Croix.

The tandem of Duncan, *right*, and David Robinson was an immediate hit.

Duncan instead focused on basketball while he continued to grow. He played in college at Wake Forest, where he stayed for four full seasons. He could have left sooner and been a top pick, but he had promised his mother he would earn a college degree.

He wasn't flashy. He earned the nickname "The Big Fundamental" because he tried to do everything the right way. That was just fine by the Spurs. When Robinson returned, he teamed up with the rookie to turn San Antonio into an NBA powerhouse.

The Spurs went from 20 wins the year before they picked Duncan to 56 wins in his first season. Duncan averaged 21.1 points, 11.9 rebounds, and 2.5 blocks. A year later, Duncan and Robinson won the NBA title, the first of five Duncan captured during his career.

04

Shaquille O'Neal's dunking ability rocked rims all over the NBA.

SHAQUILLE O'NEAL

The early years for the Orlando Magic were rough. Though fans in central Florida came out to watch the new team, they didn't see many victories during the Magic's first three seasons.

The arrival of Shaquille O'Neal in 1992 changed all that. At 7 feet 1 inch and 300 pounds, O'Neal sure was big. But his size wasn't the only thing that made "The Diesel" special.

O'Neal was long enough to swat shots out of the air and swallow up rebounds. He was quick enough to get out on the fast break. And he could dunk. During his college days at Louisiana State University, he broke the rim after one slam. O'Neal didn't take it any easier on the rims and backboards in the NBA. He spent his rookie season testing hoops all over the country.

During one game, O'Neal dunked so hard the entire basket sank to the ground. Later in the year, one of his slams sent the hoop crashing down on his head.

O'Neal's first year proved to be a smashing success. He averaged 23.4 points, 13.9 rebounds, and 3.5 blocks for the Magic. Orlando posted its best record yet at 41–41. O'Neal won the NBA Rookie of the Year Award, made the All-Star team, and became one of the league's most popular players.

HOOPS AND HOLLYWOOD

Shaquille O'Neal's appeal spread far beyond the basketball court. During his first years in the NBA, he made several rap albums and tried his hand at acting. In the movie *Kazaam*, O'Neal played a giant genie who grants wishes to a young boy. In *Blue Chips*, he starred as a high school basketball player lured to a big-time college that had fallen on hard times.

03

Rookie Larry Bird displays his moves around the basket against the Atlanta Hawks.

LARRY BIRD

In the 1978 NBA Draft, Bird was the word for the Boston Celtics. The late 1970s found the once-proud Celtics in the middle of a rough patch. They needed a player to help them turn things around. They took a chance with the sixth pick in the 1978 draft, selecting forward Larry Bird from Indiana State University.

Boston drafted Bird even though he planned to stay in college one more season to fulfill a promise to his mother. The wait turned out to be worth it for both sides.

Bird helped tiny Indiana State University reach the national championship game in 1979. The Sycamores lost to Michigan State University and its star point guard, Earvin "Magic" Johnson. But despite the loss, Bird was named the college player of the year.

As a rookie, Bird led the Celtics to the playoffs, where he matched up with superstar Julius Erving, *right*, and the 76ers.

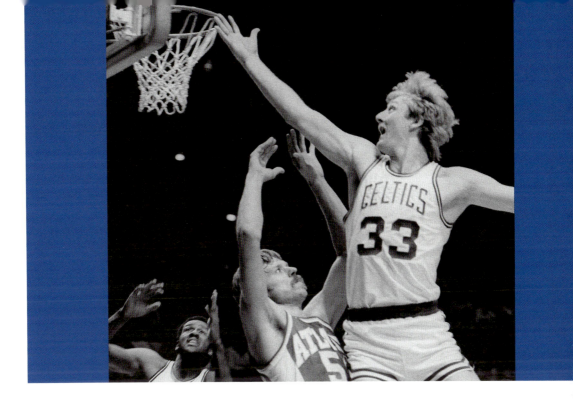

The player they called "Larry Legend" was just getting started. Bird arrived in Boston in the fall of 1979. Suddenly the magic was back at Boston Garden. Bird played small forward but could pass like a point guard, sink jumpers like a shooting guard, and rebound like a center.

His skillful all-around play keyed Boston's return to glory. The Celtics improved from 29–53 the season before Bird arrived to 61–21 during his rookie year. It marked the biggest improvement from one season to the next in NBA history.

Bird won the Rookie of the Year Award and made the All-NBA first team, meaning he was considered one of the five best players in the league.

Though Boston lost to Philadelphia in the second round of the 1980 playoffs, the Celtics were ready to take flight with Bird. Boston won three NBA titles during the 1980s, and the team retired his No. 33 shortly after his career ended in 1993.

02

OSCAR ROBERTSON

Oscar Robertson will go down in history as the man who made the triple-double cool. When a basketball player reaches double digits in three statistical categories in one game—usually points, rebounds, and assists—it's called a triple-double. It was a rare feat in the early days of the NBA. Back then, guards such as Robertson mostly just passed the ball or shot from the outside. There weren't a lot of chances to pick up rebounds, which were usually gobbled up by forwards and centers.

Robertson changed everything. Robertson was a good shooter and passer. But at 6 feet 5 inches tall, he also could get in the paint and battle with the big boys under the hoop.

Robertson starred in college at the University of Cincinnati. The NBA's Cincinnati Royals made sure Robertson didn't go far when he turned pro, taking him in the 1960 draft. "The Big O" wasted no time proving he could do it all. Robertson posted a triple-double in his first NBA game, scoring 21 points, grabbing 12 rebounds, and dishing out 10 assists in a win over the Los Angeles Lakers.

Robertson made the NBA All-Star Game as a rookie. Playing against the best players in the world, Robertson put on a show. He was named the game's MVP after finishing one assist shy of another triple-double.

Oscar Robertson, *center*, draws the close attention of Lakers star Jerry West, *left*, in a 1961 game.

TRIPLE TROUBLE

Oscar Robertson's finest statistical season came during his second year in the league, 1961–62. He became the first player in NBA history to average a triple-double over a full season, posting 30.8 points, 12.5 rebounds, and 11.4 assists per game. No NBA player did it again until Oklahoma City star Russell Westbrook did it for the Thunder in 2016–17.

01

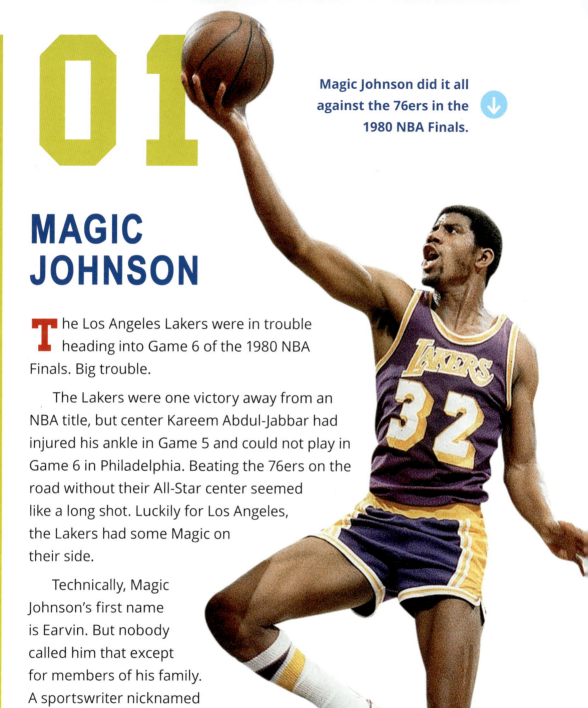

Magic Johnson did it all against the 76ers in the 1980 NBA Finals.

MAGIC JOHNSON

The Los Angeles Lakers were in trouble heading into Game 6 of the 1980 NBA Finals. Big trouble.

The Lakers were one victory away from an NBA title, but center Kareem Abdul-Jabbar had injured his ankle in Game 5 and could not play in Game 6 in Philadelphia. Beating the 76ers on the road without their All-Star center seemed like a long shot. Luckily for Los Angeles, the Lakers had some Magic on their side.

Technically, Magic Johnson's first name is Earvin. But nobody called him that except for members of his family. A sportswriter nicknamed him "Magic" while watching Johnson overwhelm the opposition

Johnson, *left*, and Bird renewed their rivalry in the NBA, meeting for the first time in December 1979.

during a high school game in Michigan. The name stuck. It helped that Johnson could do things on the basketball floor that few others could do.

Though he grew to 6 feet 9 inches tall, Johnson played guard during his college career at Michigan State University. As a sophomore, he helped guide the Spartans to the national title over Indiana State and Larry Bird.

Johnson wasn't sure he wanted to go to the NBA in 1979, but he made up his mind after the Lakers won a coin flip with Chicago for the rights to the No. 1 pick. "The only reason I came out was to play with Kareem and the Lakers," Johnson said.

Johnson had many reasons to flash his trademark smile as the Lakers took on the 76ers.

An NBA dynasty was born. Johnson proved to be the missing ingredient on a team that already had Abdul-Jabbar, forward Jamaal Wilkes, and guard Norm Nixon.

Johnson averaged 18.0 points, 7.7 rebounds, and 7.3 assists per game as the Lakers finished with the best record in the Western Conference. Then they marched to the NBA Finals for the first time since 1973.

The Lakers were in pretty good shape until Abdul-Jabbar hurt his ankle in the fourth quarter of Game 5. On the trip from Los Angeles back to Philadelphia, Johnson did his best to tell his teammates everything was going to be okay. Johnson sat in Abdul-Jabbar's usual seat on the team plane. He even told the rest of the Lakers, "never fear, EJ is here."

Turns out, Johnson was right. His versatility allowed coach Paul Westhead to play him at any position on the court. With the Lakers in need of help at center against the Sixers in the finals, Westhead decided to put Magic in the middle.

The decision led to one of the greatest performances in NBA playoff history. Johnson even jumped the opening tip against Philadelphia's 6-foot-11 center, Caldwell Jones.

Jones won the tip. That's about as good as it got for the 76ers. Johnson tied up burly Philadelphia forward Darryl Dawkins the first time the Sixers had the ball. It was Johnson's way of saying the Lakers weren't scared of Philadelphia, even without Abdul-Jabbar.

Johnson ended up playing every position during the game, finishing with 42 points, 15 rebounds, and 7 assists. The Lakers won 123–107 to clinch the first of five titles they would capture during Johnson's career.

It was a Magical night indeed for the greatest rookie in NBA history.

HONORABLE MENTIONS

ELGIN BAYLOR: The small forward averaged 24.9 points and 15.0 rebounds per game with the Minneapolis Lakers in 1958–59.

WILT CHAMBERLAIN: "Wilt the Stilt" set rookie records for points (37.6) and rebounds (27.0) per game for the Philadelphia Warriors in 1959–60. He didn't crack our Top 10 because he spent a year playing for the Harlem Globetrotters between college and the NBA.

PATRICK EWING: After a standout college career at Georgetown, the 7-foot center became a star for the New York Knicks. He was an All-Star as a rookie in 1985, averaging 20.0 points and 9.0 rebounds a game.

BLAKE GRIFFIN: A knee injury delayed Griffin's first season with the Los Angeles Clippers by a year. He returned for the 2010–11 season better than ever. He was named Rookie of the Year and flew over a car to win the Slam Dunk Contest during All-Star weekend.

ELVIN HAYES: "The Big E" led the NBA in scoring in 1968-69, averaging 28.4 points per game as a rookie with the San Diego Rockets.

HAKEEM OLAJUWON: As a rookie, "Hakeem the Dream" scored 20.6 points, grabbed 11.9 rebounds, and blocked 2.7 shots per game while teaming with Ralph Sampson to form the Twin Towers for the Houston Rockets in 1984–85.

DAVID ROBINSON: "The Admiral" came to San Antonio in 1989 after spending two years in the Navy. The Spurs improved from 21 wins the year before the 7-foot-1 center arrived to 56 wins with Robinson patrolling the middle.

RALPH SAMPSON: The 7-foot-4 center averaged 21.0 points, 11.1 rebounds, and 2.4 blocks for Houston in 1983–84.

CHRIS WEBBER: Fresh off starring with the University of Michigan's famed "Fab Five," Webber helped the high-flying Golden State Warriors reach 50 wins for the fourth time in franchise history in 1993–94.

GLOSSARY

ASSIST
A pass that leads directly to a scored basket.

CENTER
Usually the tallest player on a basketball court; typically plays close to the basket on both offense and defense.

DRAFT
A system that allows teams to acquire new players coming into a league.

DRAFT LOTTERY
A system used by the NBA to help randomly determine where teams will pick in the draft.

DUNK
To jam the ball through the hoop with one or two hands.

EXPANSION TEAM
A new team that joins an existing league.

FORWARD
A bigger player who is versatile and can both rebound and shoot.

GUARD
Usually a smaller player who can shoot from long range and pass the ball to teammates.

REBOUND
To catch the ball after a shot has been missed.

MORE INFORMATION

ONLINE RESOURCES

To learn more about great NBA rookies, visit abdobooklinks.com. These links are routinely monitored and updated to provide the most current information available.

BOOKS

Bryant, Howard. *Legends: The Best Players, Games, and Teams in Basketball*. New York: Philomel Books, 2017.

Ervin, Phil. *Total Basketball*. Minneapolis, MN: Abdo Publishing, 2017.

Graves, Will. *NBA's Top 10 Teams*. Minneapolis, MN: Abdo Publishing, 2018.

PLACE TO VISIT

NAISMITH MEMORIAL BASKETBALL HALL OF FAME
1000 Hall of Fame Avenue
Springfield, MA 01105
413-781-6500
hoophall.com

The Basketball Hall of Fame is like a museum dedicated to basketball. It highlights the greatest players, coaches, and moments in the sport's history. Many of the players mentioned in this book are enshrined there. It is home to more than 300 inductees and more than 40,000 square feet of basketball history.

INDEX

Abdul-Jabbar, Kareem, 12–13, 24, 26–27
Akron, Ohio, 8

Bellamy, Walt, 10–11
Bird, Larry, 20–21, 25
Brown, Kwame, 9

Chamberlain, Wilt, 10–11

Dawkins, Darryl, 27
Duncan, Tim, 16–17

Erving, Julius, 14

Howard, Dwight, 9

Iverson, Allen, 6, 7

James, LeBron, 8, 9
Johnson, Ervin "Magic," 20, 24–27
Jones, Caldwell, 27
Jordan, Michael, 6, 14–15

Melchiorre, Gene, 7
Mikan, George, 10, 11

New York, New York, 13
Nixon, Norm, 27

O'Neal, Shaquille, 18, 19

Robertson, Oscar, 10, 22, 23
Robinson, David, 16, 17
Russell, Bill, 10, 11

Smith, Dean, 14
Sports Illustrated, 8
St. Croix, US Virgin Islands, 16

West, Jerry, 10
Westbrook, Russell, 23
Westhead, Paul, 27
Wilkes, Jamaal, 27

ABOUT THE AUTHOR

Will Graves has spent more than two decades as a sportswriter for several newspapers and the Associated Press, covering the NFL, MLB, the NHL, and the Olympics. He's also authored more than a dozen children's sports books. He lives in Pittsburgh, Pennsylvania, with his wife and their two children.